A
LICENSE
to CHILL

Published by Advantage, Charleston, South Carolina.
Member of Advantage Media Group.

ADVANTAGE is a registered trademark and the Advantage colophon is a trademark of Advantage Media Group, Inc.

Printed in the United States of America.

ISBN: 978-1-60194-022-3

Most Advantage Media Group titles are available at special quantity discounts for bulk purchases for sales promotions, premiums, fundraising, and educational use. Special versions or book excerpts can also be created to fit specific needs.

For more information, please write: Special Markets, Advantage Media Group, P.O. Box 272, Charleston, SC 29402 or call 1.866.775.1696.

A LICENSE to CHILL

Nuggets of Truth to Encourage the Heart

Steve Gilliland

INTRODUCTION

My passion is to bring laughter to people while slipping simple nuggets of truth into their hearts, giving them courage to take a look at their challenges, and enabling them to begin to conquer them. At Steve Gilliland, Inc., our vision is to improve every situation by doing ordinary things better than anyone else and consistently demonstrate that everything we do matters.

Our purpose is to encourage and lift up other people
so they are in some way better because of the way
we lived. *A License to Chill* is from my heart to yours.
I trust it will impact you in a very positive way.

— STEVE GILLILAND

Do not be anxious about anything, but in everything, by prayer and petition, with thanksgiving, present your requests to God.

— PHILIPPIANS 4:6

It's not the mountains we conquer, but ourselves.

— EDMUND HILLARY

If you can dream it you can do it.
Dream one size bigger!

It's not how you start or how you finish.
The true joy of life is in the trip.
Enjoy The Ride!

— STEVE GILLILAND'S MANTRA

I can accept failure; everyone fails at something. But I can't accept not trying.

— MICHAEL JORDAN

Live more for today, less for tomorrow,
and never about yesterday.

There is no mistake as great as the mistake of not going on.

— WILLIAM BLAKE

Your day goes the way the
corners of your mouth go.

It ain't over till it's over.

— YOGI BERRA

When the past tries to dominate your thoughts, let your dreams ignite your day.

Remember you will not always win. But there is...always tomorrow – after you have done your best to achieve success today.

— MAXWELL MALTZ

A star shines the most when it is the darkest.

You don't have any problems.
All you need is faith in God!

— R. W. SCHAMBACH

A closed mouth gathers no feet.

I've never seen a monument
erected to a pessimist.

— PAUL HARVEY

Adversity will help you decide
what you really believe.

Why not go out on a limb?
Isn't that where the fruit is?

— FRANK SCULLY

Your mind will give back exactly
what you put in it.

Most people are only one idea, one dream, or one person away from their miracle.

— BOB HARRISON

Abundance is the result of
appreciation, not accumulation.

Life is not a dress rehearsal -
every day is opening night.

— PETER DANIELS

Give without remembering.
Receive without forgetting.

Never try to teach a pig to sing. It wastes your time and annoys the pig.

— VAN CROUCH

Never complain about what you permit.

You can make more friends in two months becoming interested in other people than you can in two years by trying to get other people interested in you.

— DALE CARNEGIE

Life is hard, but God is good.

It's what you learn after you
know it all that counts.

— JOHN WOODEN

Your options are to complain or to look ahead
and figure out how to make the situation better.

Character is what a person is in the dark.

— D. L. MOODY

We are responsible for what happens
to us, not anyone or anything else.

Lord, deliver me from the man who never makes a mistake, and also from the man who makes the same mistake twice.

— DR. WILLIAM J. MAYO

Hurting people hurt people.

You can spend your life anyway you want to, but you can only spend it once.

— DWIGHT THOMPSON

Never be content with someone
else's definition of you.

The dictionary is the only place that
success comes before work.

— VINCE LOMBARDI

By chasing "there" you can't appreciate "here."

There's no reason to be the richest man in the cemetery. You can't do any business from there.

— COLONEL SANDERS

Every little quit hurts.

Even if you're on the right track, you'll get run over if you just sit there.

— WILL ROGERS

Life provides every opportunity to get it right.

Many people fail in life because they believe in the adage: "If you don't succeed, try something else."

— DON B. OWENS, JR.

Wisdom is remembering what you already know.

Never let the fear of striking
out get in your way.

— BABE RUTH

To laugh is human, at yourself is divine.

You are the same today that you are going to be in five years from now except for two things: the people with whom you associate and the books you read.

— CHARLIE "TREMENDOUS" JONES

Do what you value. Value what you do.

Success, real success, in any endeavor demands more from an individual than most people are willing to offer – not more than they are capable of offering.

— JAMES ROCHE

If you're all wrapped up in yourself,
then you're overdressed.

God created the world out of nothing,
and as long as we are nothing, He
can make something out of us.

— MARTIN LUTHER

Sow a habit, reap a character.

A man is not old until regrets
take the place of dreams.

— JOHN BARRYMORE

The best things to hold onto in
this life are each other.

Truth is always strong, no matter how weak it looks, and falsehood is always weak no matter how strong it looks.

— MARCUS ANTONIUS

What comes from the heart goes to the heart.

It makes all the difference in the world whether we put truth in the first place or in the second place.

— JOHN MORLEY

If you're in a hole, stop digging.

Faith is like a flashlight:
no matter how dark it gets, it will help you
find your way. Every tomorrow has two
handles; we can take hold by the handle
of anxiety or by the handle of faith.

— SOUTHERN BAPTIST BROTHERHOOD JOURNAL

The best place to start is where you are today.

Keep your eye on the road, and use your rear-view mirror only to avoid trouble.

— DANIEL MEACHAM

Like your job, love your family.

Come to me, all you who are weary and burdened, and I will give you rest.

— MATTHEW 11:28

No one can ruin your day
without your permission.

The man who complains about the way the ball bounces is likely the one who dropped it.

— LOU HOLTZ

Life picks on everyone. Don't take it personally.

There is no finish line.

— Nike Corporation

The key to a long marriage is
being happy, not right.

The real glory is being knocked to your knees and then coming back.

— VINCE LOMBARDI

You will never regret your silence.

When you come to the end of your rope, tie a knot and hang on.

— FRANKLIN D. ROOSEVELT

Rejection is not fatal; it is merely someone's opinion.

The best way to cheer you up is
to cheer everybody else up.

— MARK TWAIN

Attitudes are contagious.
Make sure yours is worth catching.

You will become as small as your controlling desire; as great as your dominant aspiration.

— JAMES ALLEN

Weeds are part of life.

When you're green you're growing.
When you're ripe you're not.

— RAY KROC

Your best journey is inward.

Nothing is particularly hard if you
divide it into small jobs.

— HENRY FORD

Patience is acquired through
opportunities to exercise it.

The only way to get the best of
an argument is to avoid it.

— DALE CARNEGIE

If you don't believe in yourself,
very few other people will.

I will not provide the rope for my own lynching.

— CLARENCE THOMAS

Things crumble with the erosion of values.

Don't ever talk until you know
what you're talking about.

— SAM RAYBURN

Don't ever talk until you know
what you're talking about.

— SAM RAYBURN

We get good at whatever we practice.

The time is always right to do what is right.

— MARTIN LUTHER KING, JR.

Most of the failings of Biblical leaders
were spiritual rather than tactical.

We trust, sir, that God is on our side. It is more important to know that we are on God's side.

— ABRAHAM LINCOLN

Any bitterness in your heart will only hurt you.

Imagination is more important than knowledge.

— ALBERT EINSTEIN

You will never correct what you
are unwilling to confront.

If you want a place in the sun, you have to put up with a few blisters.

— ABIGAIL VAN BUREN

A wish changes nothing. A decision
changes everything.

Things which matter most must never be at the mercy of things which matter least.

— GOETHE

Comparison prohibits you from
seeing your uniqueness.

Success in life comes not from holding a good hand, but from playing a poor hand well.

— DENIS WAITLEY

Flexibility is when "what is" evolves
immediately into "what was."

More men fail through lack of
purpose than lack of talent.

— BILLY SUNDAY

Nothing happens without well-timed reminders.

It is better to fail in originality than
to succeed in imitation.

— HERMAN MELVILLE

Yesterday's debris clutters tomorrow's dreams.

If you're not sure where you are going,
you'll probably end up someplace else.

— ROBERT F. MAGER

Without setbacks there are no comebacks.

If we live truly, we shall truly live.

— RALPH WALDO EMERSON

If you don't like what you're getting,
change what you're doing.

God never built a Christian strong enough
to carry today's duties and tomorrow's
anxieties piled on top of them.

— THEODORE LEDYARD CUYLER

Give the man you'd like to be a
look at the man you are.

— EDGAR GUEST

Opportunity always looks bigger
going than coming.

You'll find that life is an uphill battle for the person who's not on the level.

— JOAN WELSH

We are what we repeatedly do.

We don't need more strength or more ability or greater opportunity. What we need is to use what we have.

— BASIL WALSH

You will never go above a line
until you first draw one.

If you refuse to accept anything but the best, you very often get it.

— W. Somerset Maugham

Time is irreversible and irreplaceable.

A day hemmed in prayer is less likely to unravel.

— PAT WISE

(Steve Gilliland's Mother)

Instead of taking prayer out of something, put it before everything.

People judge you by your actions, not your intentions. You may have a heart of gold, but so does a hard-boiled egg.

— MARGARET SHANNON

(Steve Gilliland's Secretary)

A pessimist is a person who, regardless of the present, is disappointed in the future.

With good judgment, little else matters.
Without it, nothing else matters.

— NOEL TICHY

Quitting is a permanent solution
to a temporary problem.

What lies behind us and what lies before us are tiny matters compared to what lies within us.

— WALT EMERSON

If things go wrong, don't go with them.

A successful person is one who can build a firm foundation with the bricks others have thrown at them.

— DAVID BRINKLEY

There is no wrong side of a bed. We get up on the wrong side of our mind.

Our attitude towards things is likely to be
more important than the things themselves.

— A.W. TOZER

What really matters is what
happens in us, not to us.

Others can stop you temporarily, but you're the only one who can do it permanently.

— JOHN MAXWELL

Never look back unless you want to go that way.

There is no security in this life, only opportunity.

— GENERAL DOUGLAS MACARTHUR

Misery is an option!

Life is like baseball: it's 95% mental
and the other half is physical.

— YOGI BERRA

You never get ahead of anyone as long as you try to get even with them.

Always do more than is required of you.

— GENERAL GEORGE S. PATTON

Maintaining the right attitude is easier than regaining the right attitude.

Man who says it cannot be done
should not interrupt man doing it.

— CHINESE PROVERB

When opportunity knocks, a grumbler complains about the noise.

There is always a best way of doing everything.

— RALPH WALDO EMERSON

Behind every great idea is someone saying, "It won't work."

Hating people is like burning down your own house to get rid of a rat.

— HARRY EMERSON FOSDICK

Some cause happiness wherever they go; others whenever they go.

The Constitution of America only
guarantees pursuit of happiness; you
have to catch up with it yourself.

— GILL ROBB WILSON

Our dignity is not in what we
do but in who we *are*.

A critic is a man who knows the
way but can't drive the car.

— KENNETH TYNAN

The journey of a thousand miles
begins with a single step.

Happiness is a direction, not a place.

— SYDNEY J. HARRIS

Nothing is opened by mistake
more than the mouth.

Unhappiness is in not knowing what we want and killing ourselves to get it.

— DON HEROLD

Chill Out!

At lunch time, sit in your parked car with sunglasses on and point a hair dryer at passing cars. See if they slow down.

Chill Out!

Page yourself over the intercom.
Don't disguise your voice.

Chill Out!

Put decaf in the coffee maker for three weeks. Once everyone has gotten over their caffeine addictions, switch to espresso.

Chill Out!

In the memo field of all your checks,
write "Spending children's inheritance."

Chill Out!

As often as possible, skip rather than walk.

Chill Out!

With a serious look on your face, the next
time you eat out, order diet water.

No one can get your goat unless you let them know where you've tied it.

ABOUT THE AUTHOR

Steve Gilliland has helped more than 1 million people become passionate about their work and their results. His book, *Enjoy The Ride,* has been purchased by numerous organizations. For more information, please visit:

www.impactstore.com/books
Steve Gilliland
P.O. Box 30220
Winston-Salem, NC 21730
866-445-5452
steve@stevegilliland.com

OTHER BOOKS BY STEVE GILLILAND:

Enjoy The Ride – How to Experience the True Joy of Life

Mum's The Word – A Mother's Lessons in Leadership

Performance Essentials in the Workplace – A Guidebook to Inspire Action and Improve Results

To order these books, or request a catalog of Steve Gilliland's products, please visit his online store at www.impactstore.com.

To Schedule Steve to Speak at Your Next Event:

Contact his Personal Assistant, Sherry Doub
Call toll free 866-445-5452
Email Sherry at sherry@stevegilliland.com